FIRE
IN THE
SKY

L. Douglas Keeney
William S. Butler

BKF

ISBN 1-884532-21-7

Photos courtesy of The Department of Defense Still Media Records Center,
The National Archives and Records Administration, the Naval Media Records Center,
the National Aeronautics and Space Administration, and Lockheed-Martin.

Printed in Canada

Published by BKF
120 Webster Street
Louisville, Kentucky 40206
502•587•8181

The producers wish to thank:

• The USFS crew—Jim Riley and Don Farmer
• Jackie Mathis of SRS
• NAWC Point Mugu Photo Branch, especially Dwayne
  DeSalvo and Monique Hodges, and NAWC Point
  Mugu Vice Commander Captain Jack Dodd
• The Department of Defense
• Russell Egnor of the Navy's News Photo Division
• Eric DeRitis of Lockheed Martin
• Allied Signal Technical Services

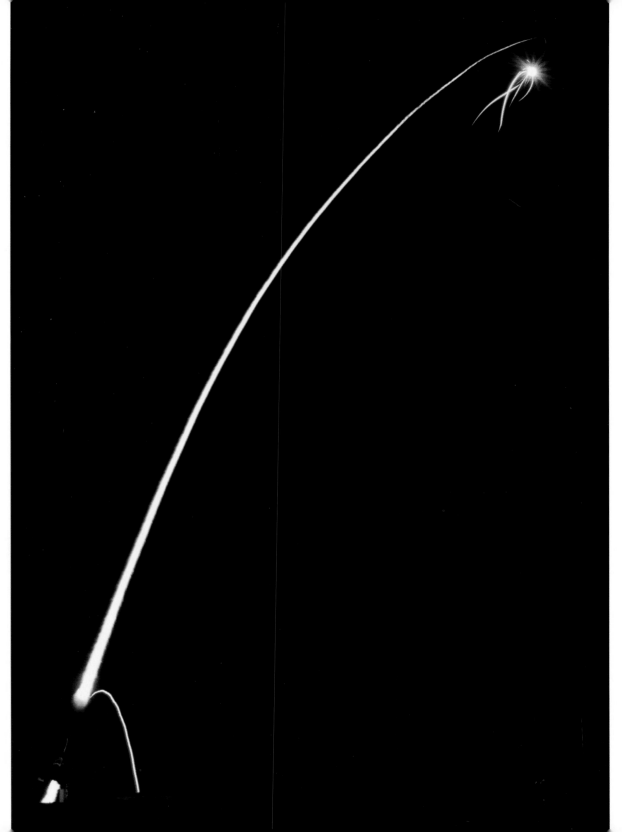

(A *MagScan* Digital Image)

8

INTRODUCTION

The basic, underlying appeal of the rocket is its audacious purpose: to overcome Nature's most powerful force—gravity—by means of a massive, controlled explosion. Unlike guns or cannons whose energy is expended in one burst of energy which depletes over distance, rocket energy overcomes gravity by means of a long, sustained burn, a self-propulsion system that fights the down-pulling forces with a complex combination of thrust and angle of attack. It's all geometry and dynamics, with a little poetry thrown in for good measure. Because when it goes as planned, a rocket's firing and flight is a visually spectacular thing. When it goes badly, the fiery result is even more spectacular.

Like all technological trial-and-error progressions, America's history with rockets is peppered with success and failure. Because modern rocket technology is a systems-based enterprise, there have always been plenty of cameras around to help in the minute analysis necessary for improvement. This has given us, the curious observer, a body of fascinating pictures, some of successes, some of blazing defeats. Fire in the Sky is an accumulation of the most interesting of these images, which as a group chronicle the milestones in rocket evolution.

Since 1940, the military uses of rockets and missiles has surely been a more vigorous and active area of research and development than the more recent and visible efforts in manned space travel. President John F. Kennedy spent more time reviewing Pershing missile tests at the White Sands Missile Range than he did observing the development of the Mercury astronaut team. The technology of ground-to-air and air-to-air missiles for military purposes has been a bustling, ongoing process; indeed, American technology in this area is considered the state of the art throughout the world.

Whether defending American shores, or fired in anger at invading aircraft, or lifting satellites into orbit, or sending astronauts to the Moon, the rocket embodies an idea of power that awes us. The science of taming that power is one of Man's noble pretensions—that he can overcome anything with the right engineering. In this area, at least, Man's pretension has been rewarded. Rocket scientists have achieved successes in every significant area of rocket power, accuracy, and overall performance.

But success has had its price. As in other risky businesses, there have been accidental deaths, especially in the astronaut corps. As a nation we have mourned, and we have learned; then we have moved on. No single tragedy will ever stop the progress of science, or divert a nation from its important business. In defense, in science, and in manned space flight, rockets and missiles play the crucial role, and until a new propulsion science is discovered, we will continue to be awed by, and fascinated with, the rocket's fire in the sky.

1940s-1960s

**The Post-War Period of
Missile Development**

Previous page: July 1948; an LTV-2 guided missile launches
from SS 348 near Point Mugu, California.

April 1948; torpedo designs are tested at the Navy's Morris Dam Lake site in
California. This test missile is being tracked by a high-speed camera.

Engineers observe both the aerodynamic and hydraulic characteristics of
the test missile as it enters the water.

Next page: The big splash as it impacts the surface of the water may
reduce the accuracy of its trajectory. A float on the lake marks its
entry point.

Above: In 1948 the Navy tested torpedo designs at this Morris Dam Lake site about twenty miles from Pasadena, California. Faster aircraft speeds made it necessary for the Navy to build a test range that could simulate the speed and angle of torpedoes dropped by low-flying aircraft. This 300-foot compressed air, fixed angle torpedo launching tube built along the shoreline would propel underwater missiles with great force into the lake.

Right: This geyser of water is hurled into the air by the entry of a torpedo into the water. The building near the water's edge houses a battery of measuring devices.

Right: Launching the LTV-N-2 #207 Loon from the Naval Test Center, Point Mugu, California, September 1950.

Both above: Sequence showing Loon Derby launch from the USS *Cusk*, June 1949.

Loon propulsion ends, and the vehicle plummets into the ocean.

Right: A "Lark" (AV-11-8) in flight from the USS Norton Sound, January 1950.

Both below: Launch photos of the #2 dummy Viking guided missile from the USS *Norton Sound* on April 22, 1950. The Naval Research Lab's guided missile group developed the Viking for the Navy after World War II. It was patterned after the German V-2, but differed in size, with a more slender shape, and a fuel tank designed into the fuselage of the rocket. Static tests began in the spring of 1949, and the first totally successful flight took place a few weeks after these photos were taken, in May 1950, also from the USS *Norton Sound*, the Navy's missile test ship.

THE JUNO II

The Juno II was a satellite launcher for the U.S. Army, using the Jupiter first stage and the Juno upper stages. It was designed in the late 1950s to carry 100 pounds into earth orbit or less weight up to lunar heights. Ten Juno II flights were undertaken between 1958 and 1961; only four performed to expectations.

A Juno II vehicle lifts off the Cape Canaveral pad in July 1959.

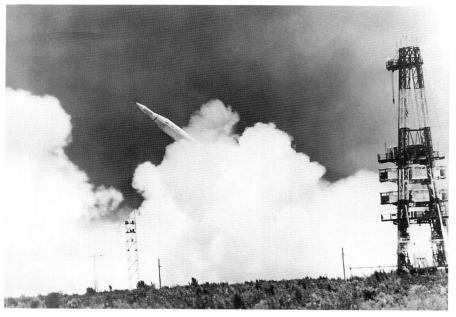

Trouble occurs almost immediately, with the rocket making a sharp left turn just barely clear of the pad. The flight lasted about five seconds before the rocket was destroyed by the range safety officer (right).

Next page: On April 7, 1950 a Lark launch from the USS *Norton Sound* was captured from a unique angle by a cameraman in a hovering helicopter.

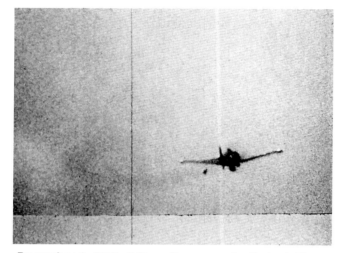

December 6, 1954. A Navy Sparrow missile test. The Sparrow was an air-to-air guided missile. Above, a target drone flies a steady course just before impact.

The Sparrow tracks and impacts the drone with a direct hit.

The drone is obliterated by the Sparrow and spins in flames to the ground.

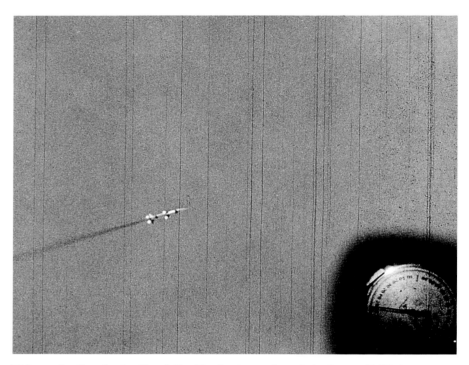

This evaluation test will ask the Terrier to seek and destroy a B-17 drone. The Terrier streaks toward its target.

A "Terrier" surface-to-air missile test gets under way from the Naval Ordnance Test Station, Inyokern, California in July 1954.

The Terrier missile can be seen homing in on the B-17 just milliseconds before impact.

The Terrier intercepts the B-17 at high speed, shearing off a wing, ending a successful test.

A Terrier guided missile fires from the left arm of an X-8 launcher at NOTS Inyokern, California in December 1952.

The Terrier tracks the target moving left to right, an F6F drone.

A successful intercept. The Terrier hits the target with full impact.

The drone plane is tracked by the Terrier...

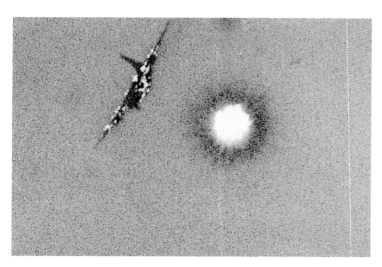

...the explosion is near enough to the target...

The Navy's supersonic anti-aircraft guided missile, the Terrier, could be launched from ground or ship to search out and destroy any type of attacking aircraft. The rocket-propelled Terrier gave the Navy a weapon of far greater lethality and range than even the largest anti-aircraft guns. This sequence took place in March 1955.

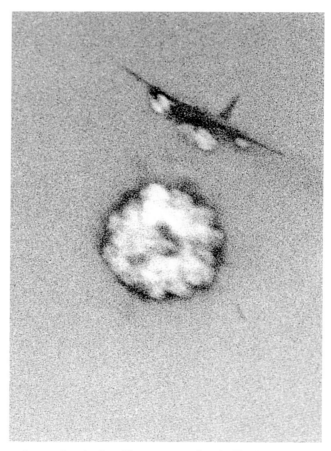

...to send a destructive concussion to the target...

...loses its wing and all structural integrity...

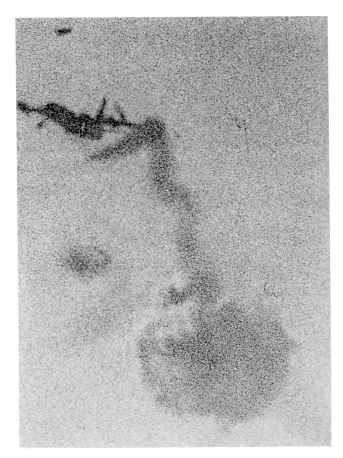

The aircraft starts to break up...

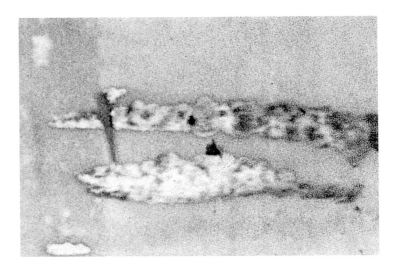

...then collapses into a fireball.

Previous page: The Navy's Regulus KDU-1 radio-controlled jet target drone being launched at NAS Chincoteague, Virginia, March 1955. The Regulus then landed on an air station runway (right), using its parachute brake, overflown by a chase plane.

A Regulus launch at Naval Air Missile Test Center Point Mugu, California, November 1950. Three chase planes keep a close eye on the launch.

In 1951, this Regulus missile lands on the dry lake beds at Muroc, California, now known as Edwards Air Force Base.

32

A chase plane photographer caught this great close-up of a Regulus in flight, October 1956.

This photo shows the proximity of the chase planes to the missile in flight.

The U.S. Air Force Northrop SM-62 "Snark" was a winged intercontinental missile powered by an Allison J-21 turbojet engine. It could deliver a 20 megaton nuclear warhead at a range of 5,000 miles, flying at supersonic speeds at altitudes over 35,000 feet. The Snark entered service in April, 1957, and was deactivated two years later when Atlas became operational.

Here at Cape Canaveral, the Snark lands after test #316, March 12, 1957.

Unsuccessful launch of an Atlas missile, test # 1002 from Pad 13, Cape Canaveral, April 14, 1959.

March 1964 was a test period for missiles fired from Point Arguello, California. These vapor trails are from a Minuteman rocket (left) and a Blue Scout rocket (right).

Rocket debris falls from the sky from an October 15, 1959 rocket failure.

Proving a jet fighter can take off from a shelter designed to withstand an atomic blast, an F-100 Super Sabre completes a zero-length launch at Holloman AFB, New Mexico, 1959.

Boiling up a dust storm in its wake an F-100 Super
Sabre leaps from its ZEL (Zero Length Launch)
platform at the Air Force's Indian Springs, Nevada
Bombing Range, May 1959.

As soon as the F-100 reached flying
speed, the rocket fell away and the
pilot performed a slow roll.

A North American F-100 performs a ZEL launch at Edwards AFB, October 1958. The F-100 reaches 275 MPH in seconds by using a solid propellant rocket to get airborne from a standing start. ZEL aircraft could be hidden underground, in woods, in shelters, or moved from place to place, and then launched on combat missions after runways had been destroyed by an attacking enemy.

An Atlas missile on Pad 11, Cape Canaveral, April 7, 1960. Atlas was the United States' first successful ICBM. Its design took advantage of the technical breakthroughs in inertial guidance and booster engine power in 1959. Atlas was a multistage, liquid oxygen-fueled rocket with three main engines, a sustainer, and two booster engines. The boost engines cut off just over two minutes after liftoff, and the sustainer continued for another three minutes to achieve a range over 10,000 miles.

At ignition, this Atlas is engulfed in flames.

Later in the same year, in August, another Atlas tries to launch, with a similar result.

Atlas missiles were deployed in hardened missile silos in the vertical position, but were fired only from above ground configurations. The Atlas was deactivated for military purposes in 1967, but the Atlas rocket was used later in the space program.

The Minuteman was an intermediate range missile with a range of 6000 miles. It was a three-stage missile, lighter and smaller than either Titan or Atlas, and carrying a smaller payload. Though smaller, the Minuteman was much less expensive to build, and therefore made up for its lack of power with sheer numbers. It was designed for launch from underground silos, but could also launch from this mobile railroad car, which, when given a radio command from the USAF Train Control Center, would head for a predetermined launch siding. The missile was held inside the car, and could be erected and launched remotely from a separate control center. This test took place in June 1960. By February 1961 the Minuteman performed its first flight, and by March 1962 it was in full service.

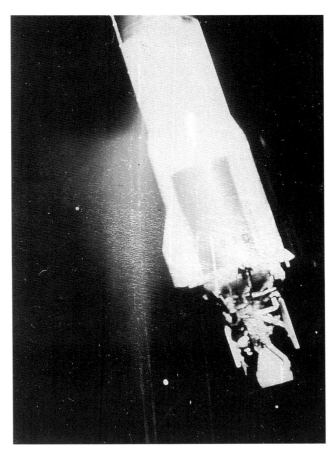

An Air Force Atlas booster, its tanks empty and rockets dead, drifts in the reentry area 650 miles above the Atlantic Missile Range, October 1960. This is among the first photographs taken from space.

At Vandenberg AFB, an advanced model Atlas blows up on the launch pad, June 7, 1961. The E series Atlas exploded three times, signalling the failure of the "coffin" launcher being tried for the first time.

Just after ignition, this SAMOS III rocket blows up on its pad at Point Arguello, California, September 1961.

November 10, 1961. An Atlas rocket has a live passenger this day, a small monkey situated in the nose cone.

Several seconds after liftoff, the rocket explodes, sending the nose cone crashing to earth.

A 76-foot-tall Juno II booster rocketed into space on February 24, 1961. Its mission was to place a satellite into orbit. Forty minutes after launch NASA was unable to confirm the firing of the upper stages of the rocket's booster. Juno II had already proved its usefulness, launching America's first successful lunar fly-by, Pioneer 4, in March of 1959.

This five-shot sequence shows a SAC Atlas ICBM blowing up on its launch pad at Vandenberg AFB just seconds after ignition, June 1961.

NASA's first Centaur research and development launch vehicle attempted to lift off from Cape Canaveral on May 8, 1962. A series of malfunctions caused it to explode, starting with the breakaway of a weather shield (picture 3), followed by the breakup of the Centaur stage (picture 4) while the booster continued to drive forward. It was only seconds before the entire vehicle was in flames (picture 5).

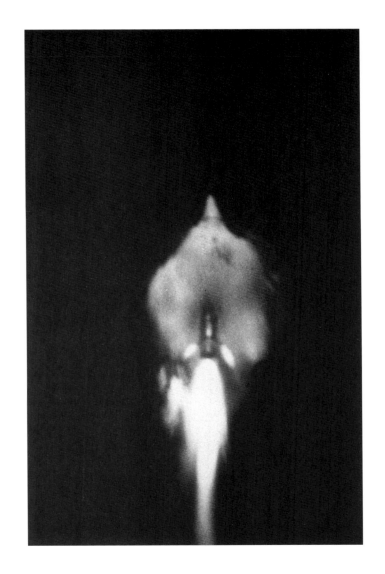 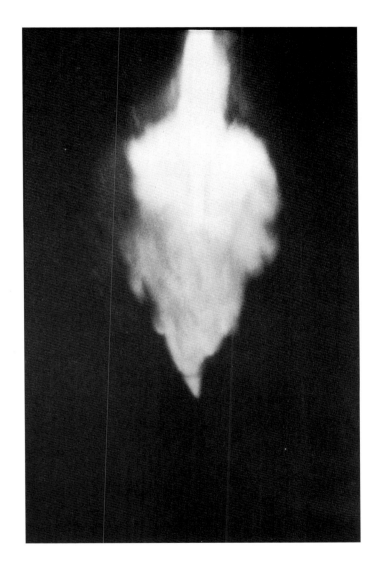

At Edwards AFB in November 1962, the X-15 rocket plane touched down on Mud Lake after an engine failure. The nose wheel broke off, causing a nose-down skid; then the aircraft skidded sideways and dug a wing into the ground, flipping over on its back. The pilot sustained minor injuries. The X-15 was the first rocket-propelled plane to come close to space altitudes. It could reach 67 miles, where thrusters were needed for control, but it could not reach earth orbit. The X-plane program ended in 1968.

The Polaris was a two-stage, solid fuel missile developed by the Navy starting in1957. It carried a nuclear warhead and could be launched from specially-designed submarines which roamed the oceans continuously throughout the Cold War. Both Presidents Eisenhower and Kennedy counted on the Polaris to be the retaliatory weapon that the Russians would respect and fear...and they were right. The first successful launching of Polaris occurred in July 1960 from the USS *George Washington*. In November 1960, the *George Washington* set out on its first operational cruise with sixteen Polaris missiles aboard.

An Apollo spacecraft dummy sits on the pad awaiting an abort test at White Sands Missile Range, New Mexico in December 1963. The escape rockets, with 155,000 pounds of thrust, could hurl the escape pod to an altitude of 4600 feet in sixteen seconds in case of an abort.

This was an essential part of the early test phase of the Apollo program, which intended to land a man on the moon within the decade.

After launch, the three ringsail parachutes landed the Apollo safely in the New Mexico desert. The descent rate of 25 feet per second left the craft unscratched.

53

Preparations are under way for a zero length launch of an F-104G at Edwards AFB in June 1963. The tensions of the Cold War produced a high state of readiness in the armed forces; it was a priority for aviation assets to get in the air quickly in case of an attack, with or without runways.

At left, the pilot climbs into the cockpit just prior to launch.

February 24, 1966. The first salvo launch of Minutemen ICBMs was made from Vandenberg AFB, California.

The Minuteman's solid propellant systems eliminated the need for cumbersome and complex loading and unloading of liquid propellants. This was the first missile that could be fired almost instantly, ushering in the era of "pushbutton" missile warfare. Minuteman silos were well emplaced in hidden locations across America by the mid-1960s. The Minuteman 3, first test-fired in 1968, had a one-ton payload, double that of the original missile.

Astronaut Neil Armstrong is at the cockpit of the lunar landing research vehicle at Ellington Air Force Base on May 6, 1968.

The LLRV is airborne, beginning an exercise that will simulate a lunar landing.

For reasons unknown, the LLRV lost power, and Armstrong used his rocket-propelled ejection seat to separate himself from the vehicle.

Armstrong's parachute floats him safely to the ground; the LLRV crashed and burned.

1970s-1990s

The Modern Era of Rocket and Missile Technology

An armored personnel carrier sits as a target for an F-4 which has just dropped an AGM-65 Maverick missile. The missile homes in on its target. The early Mavericks had a range of ten miles at sea level and up to 25 miles at altitude. These were tv-guided, air-to-ground missiles that sped to target at more than Mach 1.

The glide path indicates the target has been acquired properly. One second later the missile hits the target with devastating effect (right). Newer optics were fitted to the AGM-65B and C models, allowing target acquisition without the pilot's visual identification. An infrared seeker on the D model gives it much greater range and accuracy.

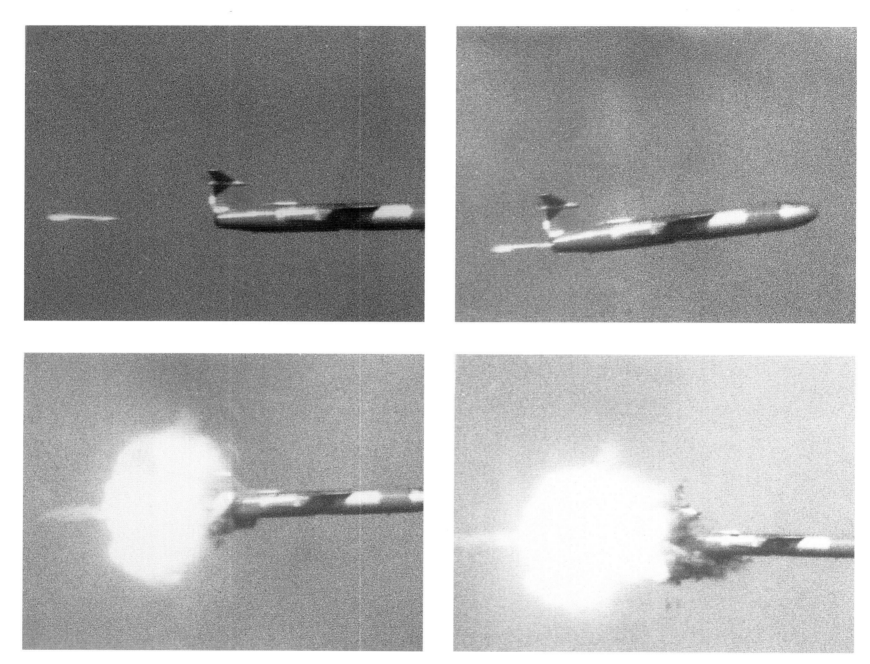

In this four-shot sequence, one of the last Mace missiles in the Air Force inventory is intercepted and destroyed by an AIM-9E during tests conducted by the 3246th Test Wing at Eglin AFB, Florida, April 1974. The Sidewinder family of AIM-9s is versatile, capable of being fitted to a wide range of aircraft. This is a short-range air-to-air missile, with a infrared sensor and a proximity-fused warhead.

This F-4D is on a bomb run to test the Modular Guided Glide Bomb (MGGB).

In the skies above Eglin AFB in Florida, August 1974, an F-4D from the 3246 Test Wing releases a rocket-propelled decoy missile (Robin) from its left wing.

The rocket moves away from the jet at supersonic speeds. The release mechanism for the missile is shown in the close-up at right.

This remarkable sequence of photographs shows a test of an Air Force MX "Peacekeeper" missile deployment method in August 1978. The MX was embroiled in some controversy regarding its launch method, with various camps arguing for either fixed, silo-type deployments or many types of mobile launch configurations. The MX shown here would be stored underground, out of sight of enemy aircraft, and upon activation its breakout mechanism would punch through ten inches of concrete and five inches of dirt, reaching launch condition in less than 60 seconds. Tests such as these near Yuma, Arizona proved that the buried trench concept of missile protection was a feasible option.

In July 1982 aerial cameras caught the flight of a Tomahawk cruise missile (in circle) approaching the starboard side of the target ship USS *Agerholm* off Point Mugu, California.

The Tomahawk finds its mark. The missile was launched from the nuclear-powered attack submarine USS *Guitarro* (SSN 665) located approximately 200 miles from the target.

A Tomahawk land-attack cruise missile is on course with its target, a concrete bunker, during a 1984 live warhead test at San Clemente Island, California. High-speed cameras caught the impact results on the following pages.

The Tomahawk, carrying a conventional payload, impacts the bunker, the nose of the missile piercing the structure.

The 1000-pound "bullpup" warhead installed in the Tomahawk detonates on impact with the target.

Launched from a submerged submarine 400 miles off the California coast, the Tomahawk used its Terrain Matching Contour (TERCON) System to find its way to the target area.

Once in the target area, the Tomahawk uses its Digital Scene Matching Area Correlator (DSMAC) to zero in on the target.

(Right) In the Gulf of Mexico, a BGM-109 Tomahawk cruise missile is launched from the battleship USS *Iowa* (BB-61) during a firing test on the Eglin AFB range, August 1986.

The Tomahawk is a medium-range cruise missile with great versatility, first deployed on Los Angeles Class submarines in early 1982.

(Left) Operation Deliberate Force in the Adriatic Sea, September 1995. A Tomahawk Land Attack Missile (T-LAM) is launched from the cruiser USS *Normandy* in the early evening hours against Bosnian Serb air defense assets in northwestern Bosnia.

The USS *Nimitz* launches a Sea Sparrow missile to destroy an incoming target drone during FLEETEX exercises, September 1995. Over 56 missiles were launched by Carrier Air Wing Nine's (CVW 9) battle group during routine training prior to a western Pacific deployment.

A Sea Sparrow missile is launched from the USS *America* (CV-66) in the Aegean Sea during Infinite Courage exercises, November 1995.

The USS *Antietam* (CG-54) launches a surface-to-air missile during missile exercises near the Hawaiian Islands.

(Left) Missile test exercises in the South China Sea, January 1996. The USS *Thatch* (FFG 43) successfully launched an MK-38 surface to air missile at an incoming target drone.

(Right) An MK-38 fires off the superstructure of the USS *Thatch*, an Oliver Hazard Perry-Class frigate.

A BGM-109 Tomahawk Land Attack Missile is launched from the forward vertical launch system aboard the guided missile cruiser USS *Bunker Hill* (CG 52) during Operation Desert Storm.

(Right) A Tomahawk lifts off from its vertical launch canister aboard the forward-deployed USS *FIFE* (DD 991). The *FIFE* successfully fired 60 vertical-launch Tomahawk missiles during Operation Desert Storm.

Navy Photo by Noel Guest

Navy Photo by Mark D. Cooper

(Left) The port-side Mark 143 armored box launcher on the stern of the nuclear-powered guided missile cruiser USS *Mississippi* (CGN-40) fires a BGM-109 Tomahawk toward its target in Iraq. The *Mississippi* fired salvos from its staging area in the Red Sea during Operation Desert Storm, January 1991.

(Above) A Tomahawk missile just after launch from the USS *Wisconsin*. Its guidance systems will take it to an impact location within several feet of the target in Iraq.

(Right) Missile away from the USS *Wisconsin*'s box launcher during Desert Storm.

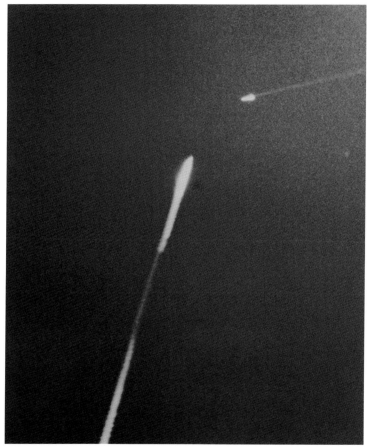

(Left) The Extended-Range Interceptor (ERINT) missile is a small hit-to-kill missile under development for possible use with the Army's Patriot missile system. Its job would be to increase defense capabilities against theater ballistic missiles. ERINT kills by kinetic energy from direct impact. Here in November 1993 ERINT is launched against a target ballistic missile re-entry vehicle.

(Above) ERINT homes in on the target vehicle approximately 14 seconds after liftoff.

(Above) ERINT successfully intercepts the target drone. This is a high-velocity impact which creates a high-energy fireball.

(Right) The vehicle and its submunition payload is destroyed by the body-to-body impact of the ERINT.

The remarkable sequence of photographs beginning here and concluding on page 89 shows how dramatic and disconcerting the underwater launch of a missile can be. To the layman, it is near-miraculous that missile engines can be fired in a liquid environment, and that an accurate trajectory can be achieved from such a sluggish start. But missile experts have known since the 1950s that underwater origination has very little impact on missile performance.

In this sequence, the underwater launch of a Tomahawk cruise missile is captured in stop-action photography taken through the periscope of the submarine. The tip of the Tomahawk is just clearing the surface of the water.

Tomahawks are versatile submarine or ship-launched subsonic cruise missiles, used to attack targets on land or sea with conventional or nuclear warheads. Solid propellants launch the missile, then give way to a turbofan engine which takes the duration of the flight cruise. Because it is small and flies at low altitudes, it is hard to spot on radar. Infrared detection is difficult because of the low heat factor of the engine. These factors make it an effective weapon, and a highly survivable missile.

The periscope view now shows the missile clearly broken through the surface.

The land-attack version of the Tomahawk is guided both inertially and with a terrain contour matching (TERCOM) system. TERCOM uses stored map references to compare with the actual terrain it sees to place the missile on course to the target. There is a global positioning system, a Digital Scene Matching Area Correlation (DSMAC) system, and Time of Arrival (TOA) control.

Milliseconds later, the Tomahawk is almost clear of the
water.

The anti-ship version of the
Tomahawk utilizes a modified
Harpoon cruise missile
guidance system. The missile
flies near its target, then at a
programmed distance begins
its active radar search to seek
out, acquire, and hit it.

The missile clears the surface and reaches its maximum flying speed of 550 mph quickly.

This missile is just over 18 feet in length and weighs just over 3,000 pounds with its booster. Its cruise range is 600 nautical miles in its conventional configuration; 1,350 nautical miles in its nuclear configuration.

Page 89: The Tomahawk speeds away from its launch site, pushed by its solid fuel booster.

A knock-down sequence featuring the Army's Hawk medium-to-high level surface-to-air missile.

The Hawk SAM system was one of the most successful air defense systems ever built. It first became operational in 1959 with the U.S. Army, then was deployed by the U.S. Marines, the NATO nations, and dozens of other countries. Over 40,000 Hawk missiles have been produced to date. By 1968 the original Hawk had been improved with a new radar and guidance package, lighter electronics, and greater range.

In the mid-to-late 1950s the push was on to develop a missile that could be stored and fired from a submarine. The primary problem to be overcome was one of accuracy; that is, how to deliver a missile to a target 1200 miles away from an unstable, moving launch platform. By 1956 an ingenious system had been developed combining the Navy's Ship Inertial Navigation System (SINS) and the inertial guidance package of the Jupiter missile, so that the position and direction of the ship would automatically be taken into account in the missile's guidance system. The missiles would, in effect, be constantly bracketed on their targets no matter what the position of the launcher.

This breakthrough made the Polaris missile possible. By 1960 the first Polaris was fired from a submerged position. Upgrades to the missile followed quickly. The A-2 and A-3 generations added range, with the A-3 approaching a 3,000-mile capability. By 1966 the U.S. missile submarine fleet was comprised of 13 subs carrying A-2s and 28 carrying A-3s.

On page 92, an A-3 Polaris is test-fired in 1964.

(A *MagScan* Digital Image)

The Nike SAM system was a fixed-base air defense system, the first guided missile system in operational use in the U.S. The initial deployment was made in 1953.

It was an Army system, and initially used the same fire-control radar used in World War II anti-aircraft systems for guidance. The intercept missile was directed to the intruder by radar, then detonated in proximity by a control computer.

At left, the original missile used in the Nike system was the Ajax. The Ajax booster pushed the missile past Mach 2 in a range of about 25 miles.

Many Nike systems were deployed in the 1950s, both in the U.S. and abroad, and because they were fixed systems using concrete and steel structures, the Army was reluctant to obsolete them, even when the Ajax missile fell into disfavor. The new Hercules missile was developed to configure with the Nike system in 1958, and offered improved performance in speed (up to Mach 3.6) and range (87 miles).

At right, a Hercules missile is launched to go after a high-flying target drone.

The Theater High Altitude Area Defense missile (THAAD), the first weapon system designed specifically to defend against theater ballistic missiles, was flown for the second time here at White Sands Missile Range in late July 1995. The Ballistic Missile Defense Organization, the U.S. Army and Lockheed were on hand to review the demonstration/validation flight, the results of which were used to either support or delay a decision to move into final design and manufacturing development.

On this day the THAAD achieved a significant portion of its flight test objectives. This particular flight tested the missile guidance and control system and its ability to respond to radar-provided target updates. The missile launched, executed the planned steering maneuver (right), separated the kill vehicle from its expended booster, and continued with mid-course guidance based on internal navigation update information.

MagScan Digital Images, both pages

The Exoatmospheric Reentry Vehicle Interceptor Subsystem (ERIS) missile is shown just after launch from Meck Island at the U.S. Army's Kwajalein Atoll in the mid-Pacific in March 1992.

The ERIS is part of the validation program under the Strategic Defense Initiative. ERIS is designed to verify key technologies for target designation, scene matching and destruction of enemy ballistic missile reentry vehicles above the earth's atmosphere.

This is the second test of ERIS, which involved the identification, tracking, and homing of a mock ballistic missile nuclear warhead and a closely-spaced decoy above the earth's atmosphere. The target and decoy were launched from Vandenberg AFB, California, more than 4,500 miles away. In this instance, ERIS missed its target, but officials were pleased that all other major goals were met.

A *MagScan* Digital Image

As guidance systems became more sophisticated during the 1980s, weapons designers were able to create precision-guided munitions (PGMs) so accurate that they could be dropped into the ceiling vents of buildings. The military advantage of this accuracy is obvious: kill efficiency with low risk is the goal of every military operation. There are other pluses: the collateral damage to non-combatants is virtually eliminated, enabling strike forces to limit the battlefield to war targets only.

Here a test PGM has followed an accurate flight path and is about to impact the concrete target bunker.

The impact velocity is approximately in the Mach 4 range. The 1,000-pound bullpup warhead causes complete destruction of the target.

This airborne towed target is designed to emit heat in the frequency spectrum which will simulate an enemy aircraft exhaust plume. An air-to-air infrared-seeking missile such as the AIM-9 Sidewinder can be fired at this target for realistic training purposes. Here the target is being reeled out, and will sit approximately 1500 meters behind the airplane.

An F/A-18 launches a Sidewinder missile from its left wing. The Sidewinder first came into service in the late 1950s and has been in continual upgrade ever since. It is arguably the most durable and long-lasting air-to-air dogfight weapon ever built.

A6 Callsign Bloodhound 55 from the Pacific Missile Test Center is on a mission to launch a BQM target drone over the Sea Range at Point Mugu, California.

The TOW long-range anti-tank missile was an American development of the mid-1960s. It is a wire-guided missile that is normally launched from a vehicle such as a Jeep or an armored personnel carrier, but there is an infantry version as well. Its velocity to target is about Mach 1. Improvements continue to be made in warhead power, range, loading, and thermal imaging for night use. A *MagScan* Digital Image

At right, an AV8B releases two SnakeEye high-drag, free-fall general purpose bombs over the land range at China Lake, California.

An A7 from the Naval Air Warfare Center China Lake launches an early version of the Harpoon missile. This is an anti-ship missile, developed in the late 1960s as a ship-launched weapon, but redesigned for air and submarine use in the early 1970s. It approaches its target at virtually sea level, but gains altitude before diving on its target ship, deliberately striking the more vulnerable upper superstructure.

An F-14 from VX-4 based at the Naval Air Warfare Center Weapons Division, Point Mugu, California, launches an AIM-7 Sparrow air-to-air missile. The AIM-7 has undergone extensive upgrades since its inception in the early 1960s, and is now more deadly than ever. A version was even developed for ship self-defense called the Sea Sparrow.

The AIM-7 radar guided Sparrow missile approaches a QF-102 target drone over the sea range at Eglin AFB, Florida.

The AIM-7 impacts its target with a direct hit.

An F-14 Callsign Bloodhound 200 from Point Mugu, California launches a Phoenix air-to-air missile. The Phoenix, guided by the AWG-9 radar, was designed to intercept six targets simultaneously up to 60 miles away.

A Navy F-111 carries an early version of the Phoenix missile to a test site. This missile was developed in the early 1960s as a standard armament of the F-111. Flight testing began in 1965, and after successful trials, was put into production in 1973.

The Phoenix has a speed over Mach 5, and a look-down radar range in excess of 150 miles. It became the standard armament for the Navy's F-14A Tomcat.

An F/A-18 from NAWC Weapons Division Point Mugu, California launches an AMRAAM over the sea range. The Advanced Medium Range Air-to-Air Missile is a Mach 4 Beyond Visual Range (BVR) weapon, designed to be less expensive but more lethal than the Sparrow.

An F-16 launches a Maverick missile at a target on the land range at China Lake, California. The Maverick was originally electro-optically guided by means of a television camera in the nose. Newer versions integrate laser guidance and IR modes in the seeker.

An IR photo of a Walleye glide bomb test hit. The Walleye was developed by the Navy in the early 1960s, and used camera guidance as the target acquisition and lock-on mechanism. This weapon was used successfully in Vietnam, often by pairs of aircraft, one to release the weapon and another to guide it to the target.

TGT   226:19:57:31.1322 91A007
FLEET WALLEYE 8/14/91 RND#2

A Vandal target (a modified TALOS missile) rises from the launch pad at the Pacific Missile Range Facility (PMRF) Hawaii. The Vandal is a remote-controlled, non-recoverable target designed to provide a realistic Mach 2 anti-ship missile threat.

The Vandal leaves the rails of the launcher. The Vandal was built originally as a surface-to-air missile, but has now been converted to an airborne target role. There are many variants of this missile, which are all now designed for fleet training.

A Harpoon Block 1D anti-ship cruise missile is launched from the USS Jouett (CG-29), a Belknap Class AAW guided missile cruiser during operations conducted at the Pacific Missile Test Center, Point Mugu, California.

A Ticonderoga Class Aegis Guided Missile Cruiser launches a surface-to-air missile during test exercises in the Pacific.

Above: An SM-2 launch.

Left: A double SM-2 launch from a Ticonderoga Class (CG-47) Aegis Guided Missile Cruiser. The Aegis Combat System was designed to provide protection for the fleet against saturation anti-ship cruise missile attack in a dense electronic warfare environment. The SM-2 is a long-range version of the Standard missile.

An SM-2 is launched from an Arleigh Burke Class (DDG 51) Guided
Missile Destroyer. The Arleigh Burke Class is made of steel with
Kevlar armor protection and has a thorough Nuclear, Biological,
Chemical Warfare decontamination system installed.

The USS Antietam (CG-54) launches a surface-to-air missile during
exercises near the Hawaiian Islands.

A Standard Missile is launched from an Oliver Hazard Perry Class FFG Frigate during a missile exercise at the Pacific Missile Test Center, Point Mugu, California. This class was originally built as the cheaper component of the fleet-wide high/low technology mix. It has since undergone many upgrades and has proven capable of accepting much new equipment.

A Tomahawk cruise missile launched from an offshore submarine approaches its target. This particular exercise was a test of the Tomahawk's ability to destroy parked aircraft in revetments by a programmed proximity airburst. At right, the effectiveness of this method is demonstrated clearly.

The battlefield of the future is being tested today. Exercises such as those shown on these pages are the evaluation grounds for whole battlefield systems, encompassing laser-guided weapons, fast-reaction ground-to-air missiles, and a whole inventory of sophisticated measures and counter-measures that utilize digital microprocessor technology.

Even the humble infantryman is taking part. He will be outfitted with personal weaponry and surveillance hardware that will allow him to see more, make better decisions, and deliver a wide range of ordnance with speed and accuracy.

Left and right: These spectacular photographs show six unarmed Multiple Independently Targeted Re-entry Vehicles (MRVs) approaching their targets on the missile range off the Kwajalein Atoll in the Pacific Ocean.

Left: The Space Shuttle, which began its initial design phase in the late 1960s, was (and still is) the vehicle that answered NASA's need for a re-useable space vehicle. For nearly five years the Shuttle's four orbiters—Columbia, Challenger, Discovery, and Atlantis—flew near-perfect missions. That all changed on this day—January 28, 1986—when the Challenger flight 51-L lifted off on a chilly day.

Below: Challenger ascends in a predictable trajectory. All systems are nominal, and ground control gives Challenger the go-ahead for throttle-up. At this moment, 73 seconds into the flight, Challenger erupts in a ball of flame.

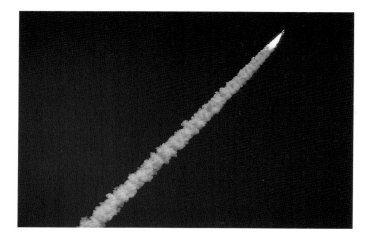

The external booster of Challenger explodes, enveloping the orbiter and setting off an instantaneous chain of major structural failures that destroyed the vehicle and its seven-person crew.

Seconds after the explosion, main engine exhaust, solid rocket booster plume and an expanding ball of gas from the external tank are visible to tracking cameras. This tragedy was thoroughly investigated, during which time the Shuttle fleet was grounded, and remained so until September 1988. It was eventually determined that cold temperatures at launch had caused an O-ring to fail, allowing booster flames to destroy a booster strut, which in turn led to structural failure. This accident made it clear that the escape system for the astronauts was ineffective during this phase of the launch. In a long string of missile failures and mishaps, including the deaths of astronauts Grissom, White and Chaffee in a flash fire in 1967, the Challenger disaster was the most devastating event in the history of America's missile program. But even this will not deter further space exploration, and many more years of fire in the sky.